# Here, We Cross

# Here, We Cross

a collection of queer and genderfluid
poetry from *Stone Telling* 1 - 7

edited by Rose Lemberg

Stone Bird Press

Lawrence, KS

Editor:  Rose Lemberg

Layout and Production:  Jennifer Smith

Cover Design:  Rose Lemberg

using "Kibirkštys III" by Mikalojus Konstantinas Čiurlionis


ISBN:  0615641393
ISBN-13:  978-0615641393

To the Secret Poetry Cabal:

Community is not everything, but it is the next best thing.

# A Table of Contents

# Acknowledgements

Many heartfelt thanks to Julia Rios, whose work at Outer Alliance is inspiring, and at whose suggestion this chapbook came into being. She is also a tireless interviewer at Stone Telling, whose acute questions and observations facilitate consistently wonderful and necessary roundtable discussions. I would like to thank Shweta Narayan, my co-editor and partner in crime – though she could not participate in the making of this chapbook due to health related issues, her work is nevertheless apparent in it. My thanks to Alex Dally MacFarlane for giving this chapbook a title. And last but not least, I would like to express my sincerest gratitude to Jennifer Smith, who worked tirelessly on the book's physical shape, and without whose perseverance and enthusiasm this book would not exist.

*Rose Lemberg*

# Introduction

A bridge is built. A bridge is built over turbulent water. A bridge is built over emptiness. Even if the bridge falls down, the memory of that bridge remains: here, we crossed. Here we stood, looking down into wordlessness, and gave it a name.

In a recent essay on growing up queer in the Soviet Union, I wrote,

> Silence is not about choosing not to speak out, silence is the lack of language in which to speak out, the impossibility of even rudimentary understanding of the self — understanding that must come before action, before reconciliation, before everything. The first issue of *Stone Telling*, 'Silence to Speech', was addressing that in part — a recognition that not just me, but many other people move in silences, are erased, are gathering courage to speak — and poetry is such a powerful vehicle for this.

Since the inception of *Stone Telling*, I – and later, Shweta and I – have been looking for queer poetry – asking for it, reaching out to poets, celebrating when such submissions landed in the inbox. And yet, we've been concerned by how little of it there was – both in *Stone Telling* and in the field in general, especially given how many speculative poets identify as queer. Clearly, the issue wasn't that of overt homophobia, but rather that of silence, a lack of discourse that translated into a scarcity of works in which the queer element was overtly expressed. Thus, the idea of 'Bridging: The Queer Issue' (*Stone Telling* 7) was born. And after that issue was published, I decided to collect all queer and genderfluid poems from issues 1 - 7 into a special edition chapbook, which you are now holding in your hands.

*Here, We Cross* is a celebration of poetry that is as diverse and varied as the *Stone Telling* audience and contributors. Here you will find poems with speakers or protagonists who are lesbian, gay, bisexual, genderqueer, trans*, asexual, and neutrois; speakers who struggle with the body and the society's imposed readings of that body. These poems have been written by queer-identified people, by allies, and by people who are, for a variety of reasons, not ready to openly speak of their queerness. There is a variety of genres in this book, including fantasy, science fiction, steampunk, magic realism, surrealism/slipstream, and poems verging on the non-speculative.

The chapbook's title is *Here, We Cross*, but it is, perhaps, not enough to cross only once. Though the bridge may be a static thing, the act of crossing changes us. We may yearn for a distant land the bridge can take us to; once there, we may perhaps feel eager to return. Here, we cross – but crossing is continuous, a reaching out from silence into a spoken space, and from that spoken space to yet another. Crossing, we transform ourselves, we celebrate and acknowledge the fluid nature of identity, including but not limited to gender and sexual expression.

I am immensely proud of the work collected here, of the brave and raw voices that speak their stories of love, pain, transformation, and triumph. It is my hope that these poems will inspire and empower others to speak what is in their hearts and to know that in this work, they are not alone. Perhaps appropriately, *Here, We Cross* is the first title published by Stone Bird Press. May it be the first of many.

# Here, We Cross

*Alex Dally MacFarlane*

## Sung Around Alsar-Scented Fires

**Under Falna's Mask:**
See me! See me! Falna the fierce
with my son on my back, tenth child, battle-charm;
with my wife at my side, her hair bare of bones
and her knife sharp as anger.
My hair is full.
Hear me! My hair clacks out
the names of the dead, speaks their existence
in toe-bones that still smell of burnt alsar.

> *Singers:*
> *See the bones in her hair!*
> *How they sing out the names of the dead!*

See the stars in the sky — how they shine!
How they spit out bright craft of silver and white and
people from far away,
wanting our land for tests, for farms, for factories,
for the gold that runs through it like solidified rivers —
our wealth. *Ours.*

They found my family.

> *Sing: Tuvi, Cira, Fari, Fa-qaro, Fa-sen!*

The wind blew bare of their names,
forgetful. No one knew of their deaths
until I
came home. Hear me!

> *Sing: Tuvi, Cira, Fari, Fa-qaro, Fa-sen!*
> *How the wind carries them here!*

Hear me sing their names: Tuvi, Cira, Fari, Fa-qaro, Fa-sen!
I sang as I neatened their bodies, laid under the sky
properly, accidentally — the far-off people gave them that,
but no one burnt alsar at their feet,
no one spoke a name,
not one.
No one wept into a wife's shoulder,
strong as love.  No one took bones for hair-ornament
and strapped a tenth child to a back, for luck,
for victory,
until I did those things.  Hear me!

> *See the knife in her hand!*
> *How it calls out for vengeance in blood!*

In a camp, in tents white as hot metal,
as their weapons that burned through my family's flesh —
only six of them lived, fever's first flush.
We wielded surprise.
We rode into their camp, two to a befil
and our son on my back; we offered trade,
gold for medicine.  My wife coughed.
My wife struck first, when they turned their backs
like chives under a blade.

> *Sing: Tuvi, Cira, Fari, Fa-qaro, Fa-sen!*
> *How the wind remembers them there!*

Like chives, un-sung, they fell.  They bloodied the ground
and we covered them with stones,
un-buried.  We didn't learn their names.
We left,

2

our cheeks tattooed with victory
our son's tattooed with luck:
a single black line, horizon-straight.

But hear me!

> *See the dead on the ground!*
> *How they fall, though we stand and fight!*

More will come,
dead-collecting, dead-avenging,
holding excuses like blades.
See me!  Falna the fierce —
their weapons didn't kill us!

> *See Falna the fierce!*
> *How her bones are like tenth-child charms —*
> > *capricious.*

> *See the far-off people's craft!*
> *How they fly like chives re-growing.*

*Nancy Sheng*

## Inner Workings

*The Mechanical Turk was a chess-playing automaton exhibited in the late 18th century. Proclaimed a marvel and a curiosity, it was later exposed as a human.*

Yes, I said,
my voice tangled in silver and chrome.
*In all the ways, yes, yes,*
*I learn to break myself.*

First I considered the rook. (Many do).
My fingers were long like pistons.
Then I considered the bishop. (As you do).
My eyes were sealed shut with steam.
Finally I considered the queen and the king,
and my opponent sliced his lady across the board
in the manner of a knife falling over my head,
my throat laid bare by copper wires.
All of this, and for five shillings,
you too can see my metal body turn.

*The Mechanical Turk, live in exhibition!*
*Is it a man? Is it a woman? Is it a wonder?*

This is the curious thing about wonders:
No one wonders what they do when the hours pass
and the grand buildings fold on themselves like forest fires,
the penny boys walking through, dimming all the lights.

First I considered my fingers,
and then I took them off, one by one.
Then I considered my eyes,

—
4

and I put them in my pocket for safekeeping.
Finally I considered my head and my throat,
which I wrapped in butcher paper on the highest shelf.
My body moves two spaces forward, one space right.
My body is the pawn that has crossed the chequered sea.

I go dancing.

(After a long day of castling).

I go dancing.

And they will say to me:
(Sir, madam, sir, madam)
Are you king or are you queen?
And I will touch the shape of my breasts, my hips,
before trailing my finger to the moustache above my lips.

I know: they would alter my stories in sixteen pieces,
but I have forgotten their language of enigma.
I peel myself open to look inside
at where I live, beginning, middle, end,
and there in the centre of me, waiting
*(in all the ways, yes, yes,*
*I learn to make myself)*
— a ripe human heart.

Michele Bannister

## Seamstress

I have the measurements of your very skin.
This is my integument against uncertainty:
twenty-one layers to fit your form,
spandex, nylon, mylar, and hope —
the last stitched down with ragged edges.

I must be as precise as the width of the eye of my needle,
as precise as your launch window;
you can measure the movements of the planets to millimetres,
but oh, unforgiving gravity,
and you in less than half a centimetre of my care.

This piecing for the curve of your hips;
this for the arch of your back.
Now the fiddly seams around the bust;
a crease is eighteen hours of torment.

There is such grace in every arc from pad to orbit, you tell me
and for the delight in your eyes, I will see it too —
and check the tolerances three more times. And again after lunch.

I quilt beside the cooling pipes.
This stitch will lie next to your heart;
in silken metal I add the dogwood-petal circuits
your grandmother loved.
But for the gloves, grass-green and gold,
I embroider all the flowers of our garden —

It is the aluminised gleam that catches in my eye. So bright
as acrid as the glare
when you see that first sunrise from orbit; they say the glory
of that thin layer of lightning-quilted atmosphere, excruciating blue,
is heartbreaking.

*Jack H. Marr*

## Lunectomy

Once I was branded with the swelling moon.
It sank within me and gestated there,
obscene and useless, its twin satellites
pocked moonlets
pushing out their pearl-white parasite eggs
in mute optimism.

(In the sky the true moon, curved as horns,
looked down at me; he winked.
My parasite moon began a steady leak like grief:
thick tears.  Every lunation
a bloody hell.)

At last they pulled it from within me
the slick red threads and pinkish swell of it
as ominous (as innocent) as a tumour.
An impossible birth through
opened holes
cross-shaped gills black with
spider-stitches,
through the stretched-out ache.

The true moon settled there, where it had been:
An upturned crescent fierce and white
and blazed its bull-head light.

*Shira Lipkin*

# The Changeling's Lament

I have studied so hard
to pass as one of you.
I've spent a lifetime on it.

I have tells.
Blisters, tremors, bruises,
all the signs that I was not meant for your world,
was not meant to be contained
in your clothes,
your shoes.
I have this terribly inconvenient allergy
to cold iron.
Hives, really.
Welts.
I stand out.

When I was little,
I asked my alleged mother,
*what's a girl?*

She said
*you,*
*you're a girl,*
and she laced me into dresses
(that I tore off in the school parking lot,
in line for the bus).
Laced me into ballet shoes
that left blisters
and bloodied my feet
until I had calluses.
Which she had filed off,
beauticians pinning me down,

—

because it's not beauty
if you don't bleed.

My dancing was different.
My dancing was swaying treelike,
or launching myself across the room,
spinning madly,
but that is not what girls do,
not human girls,
not ladylike,
not contained.

And everything
is about *containment*
is about being delicate
and pretty
laced into corsets
whalebone stays digging into your ribs
because it's not beauty
if it doesn't hurt.

But I studied.
I pretended.
I hid the bruises
and the tics.
I hid the big dark parts of me.
I tamed my hair.
I watched my mouth.
I hid my magic.
I did not speak of such things
because we do not speak of such things –
not anger,

not homesickness,
not longing.
Not this sense
that I don't know what the hell
a human girl is
and I can tell, I can,
that everyone knows I don't belong here.
I laugh too loud;
I am too fast or slow to laugh.
I am an anthropologist in the field of girl.
I study
but none of it
ever comes
naturally.

None of it is in my nature.

I am something larger,
more fluid,
less constrained.
But I am stranded in this place.
I have had to learn how to live here.
I have tried.
So hard.

*Dominik Parisien*

## In His Eighty-Second Year

What he sees is
    the Woodbine-covered scarecrow in the garden
    a green man crowned in violet blue, with spectacles of
            shattered glass
    an old man with a burlap suit spotted black with berries

What he hears is
    his daughter peeling covers off pill-filled containers
    water, his lungs filling and his heartbeat drowning
    a vine and leaf mouth whispering *I love you I love you I love*

What he says is
    make my blue eyes green green green
    fill my mouth with dirt, my veins with sap, my bones
            with seeds
    *I'm sorry, I am, so sorry*

What he does is
    weep for a life loathed, a life loved
    smear his face in black-brown earth, stain his shirt green
    tell his daughter who knew all along

*Bogi Takács*

## The Handcrafted Motions of Flight

The men in suits pay me to remember.
Preceding lives are not always set in the past
and causality traces meandering pathways
upon the manifold surfaces of our world.
I remember the future.

I write it all down; all the fragments
of a tenuous, incoherent lore.
My mind fills in the gaps, unbidden.

There are multiple sets of futures,
multiple lives, multiple selves.
Some are me, some only similar to myself,
and some carry more of me
than my self living and writing in the present.
Hand me another sheaf!

\*\*\*

E is the one closest to me
and e is the one who arouses their interest,
with eir memories of weapons and raw power.

They are bothered by the pronouns.
The smallest details can mean the world to me —
that landscape in the future, in a causal past
of smooth beige edges and silence.

I cannot see eir face —
There are no mirrors in the memories.
Eir chest — my chest — is smooth and flat,
eir arms muscular, eir hips wide and round.

I had to assemble everything from pieces
and I could not chance upon a gender
until I realized that was a gender in itself.

They tell me to write about warfare.

***

E was — is — I am a warrior,
but e remembers only peacetime
and the soundless crashes of training,
eir self surrounded by concepts
I cannot interpret.
E does not dwell on them.

In my mind there is only a firm touch,
a nod, the smile of a comrade,
there is only the air rushing past
and the sense of speed;
all the handcrafted motions of flight.

They ask me if I am a clone (why?)
or if I am inhuman, like a robot
built for a singular military purpose —
not as far as I can tell.
I can sense disappointment
in the voices that urge me to go on.

***

Obviously this is for the nation —
an imaginary structure of mirrors,
edifices and cufflinks.

I cannot share everything.
Inside, I still owe my allegiance
to the people beyond the haze
of imperfect reconstructions.

A moment stands out.
The balding stranger looks at me
with no internal calculations,
sees me for who I am.
Our interlocking thoughts
pass a message of trust.

***

I smile.
They look at me without suspicion
as I mangle facts with a delicate touch.

They do not sense the vertigo of inversion,
the jarring tactile sensation
of patterns shifting from place.
My hesitation is attributed to fear.
They offer assurances of safety
and I nod, earnest and sheepish.

I safeguard what is my own.
Respect offered without regard to interest,
the steady gaze of an unknown passer-by.
I have to build fortifications.

\*\*\*

I am not liked; I am useful.

A firm hand gathers the sheets,
a well-groomed head turns away.
The next day lies in wait,
with carefully misaligned lines
on blueprints more coveted
than treasuries of gold.

Despite it all, I retrieve myself.

*Hel Gurney*

Hair

I have carried my hair like a flag since the day it passed my
                                        shoulder-blades.

This is the hair of feminine indolence —
of hours sacrificed to brush and wash and dry,
of cultivated shimmer and availability:
a signal to chevaliers from high-built towers, to be guillotined at
                                        the wedding altar.
The hair of someone who goes out with *nice boys*.
This is the hair hacked off by Silence and Eugenia
and a thousand nameless others who left the jewel from the crown
                                        of their heads
and swaddled themselves in travelling-cloaks and new, rough
                                                voices.
Pantene, L'Oréal, and Garnier consider me a target market.
This is my malleable raw material, to be pinned and ribboned and
                                                curled.
Every day untended betrays the soul of womankind!

No? No.
This is the hair I hid behind in class,
newly-inked universes spiralling across my notepad.
I always drew myself with one eye covered.
When I spoke, I felt my voice echoing from a brunette cavern.
The hair which slapped across my face when I was five and
sticking my head out of the car window — a practice flight
for when I grew up and became King of the Eagles.
This is the hair my nan called a "bird's nest"
and painstakingly brushed until arthritis took her joints.
The hair that flames up copper with brown eyes in the sunset.
That has been two decades mine.

This is the hair that traps me.
The promised lands of Butch and Passing lie beyond a gate
around which these tresses twine — a lock, or two,
that lets me only look *at* the recognisably masculine.
But I am "passing" every day.
I am passing as a normal fucking woman
and it is the biggest and most terrifying lie I have lived.
I could make my life legible on it with dye and gel and clippers.
I could hack it off or spike it up or brand it rainbow.
Because what is it? Raw material for a style.
A new one every day — shorter, brighter, wilder, sterner,
with clippings left for stick-on stubble.

… No.
This is the frustrating, tangled, dirty mess that I know I can tease
                                                        into beauty.
This is memory. This is something certain.
This is the number one part of my corporeal presence that I have no
    desire to bring to an expert with sharp implements who offers to
    change my life with a few strategic incisions.
This is no-one's prize but mine — and no-one's price but mine.
This is the flag I bring to the battles of my days.

*Mary Alexandra Agner*

# Tertiary

Today I took off my breasts
for the first time, the only time,
alone in a hospital room
too embarrassed to look
at the directions the nurse had left.
No more woman, never mother,
no mere anything, anomaly.
Outside this building: crowds
and signs and jeers and hate.
Soon some slang to rob me –
of what? My sexuality
is not defined by lumps of fat.
Know me well enough to know
and I will make you moan with me.
I have made form fit function.

Formless, what can my function be?
I stepped across the line
dividing me from every living thing
when I divided self in three.
Even the aliens, in UFOs, make babies.
As though I'm outside time,
no laugh track, no loop back
for my DNA, my balance gone
as I lean forward for my shirt:
I feel the holes.
Swallow, swallow nausea, pride,
the tannin memory this was my choice.
Empty clinic, clock tick,
time enough for all the thousand
mistakes through which I make me *me*.

Mistakes never unmade me.
Even in regret, pushed through,
breasts first (since ten),
now nothing first, my knees perhaps
my nose, no longer top-heavy, tipped.
A shirt has never lain so flat.
Fear keeps it still.
More than twenty years of eyes
on chest – never one way to stop them
staring – should have pinned pinstripe
and lace in place, immovable.
Just craters now, echo by echo
changing my responsibilities:
self over generations, selfishness
that generates. A contradiction.

I generate so many contradictions:
stark naked even clothed,
armor of skin too sensitive to touch.
New body, same old me,
but now displayed for everyone
to see what I have always been:
alone, an end. Unreal.
Space is the risk of flesh
colliding, crowd recoiling,
giving hate so many names:
soulless, slut, witch, bitch,
insisting on my sex the less it shows.
Their voices shove and pull,
word-war un-verbing *woman*,
conjugating *human* into *change*.

Still human? Have I changed
so much cars honk and people slink away?
I work, I walk,
same route, same old routine,
now lonelier. Inside out
my lover doesn't recognize me,
leaves no note, nothing of note
except my broken heart –
accept my broken heart? –
too near the surface. Circus freak
in an everyday big top, big-top-less:
*tit*illate the men,
comfort the women by comparison.
No role model for tertiary.
Thesis. Antithesis. Epiphany.

This is. This isn't my epiphany,
that takes another 14 lines –
or lives – at least. I wish.
This is no fairy tale
of tinted glass and Russian dolls
although my dream came true.
I made myself a refuge and example.
Every un-mother in a mother's body
hears this call. Tradition
puts its nails to chalkboard.
Out-sing the screech:
my body is my body is my body,
when I was born, first bled
and bled again, even the day
I took off my breasts.

*Amal El-Mohtar*

## Asteres Planetai

*Ancient Greek astronomers coined the term* asteres planetai *(ἀστέρες πλανῆται), or "wandering stars", for celestial bodies which appeared to move across the sky.*

**I.**

I used to think I was a star.

I used to think
*I am only visible at night.*

I used to think
that when the world's face turned from the sun,
blinking narrow eyes at an emptied sky,
there would I be, pulsing
with my own light.

But I am not a star.

**II.**

My depths and surfaces are scored
with meteoric phrases, burning on entry,
blazing, unexpected.

*It's only a phase.*
*Disgusting.*
*Unnatural.*
*Not while you're under my roof.*

These grooves, these lakes, these hills and valleys
wander with me,
warp my weight,
tilt my axis by small degrees
that make all the difference.

In these ways, too,
I am not a star.
When the sun's beams ebb from the sky
like tidal fingers, I shine—
but still
I am not a star.

## III.

Stars, like the sun,
know their place.

Because they can trace
with beautiful precision
their distance from each other,
they demand to know
their distance from me.

I shake my head,
behold my shining feet.
I have no fixed abode.
I make my home of motion—
I cannot stand still.
And my light—

*You are a star.*
*You are like us.*
*Stay with us in the dark.*
*Everyone will see you for what you are.*

I love the dark.
But if I were to stand still in the dark
and look like a star,
I would only be half myself,
and though I yearn for them with my core
and my gravity,
and I am full, so full, of heat,
I am not a star.

**IV.**

I do not fall like stars do.
Stars fall out of place, and mourn the loss — I
fall *in* to place.
When the falling has me, I
twist my body into orbit,
make a sun of my love,
feel my face become bright with theirs.

If I love in the dark, I seem a star.
If I love in the day, I do not.

A sun, after all,
is a star
who has chosen never to be seen in the dark.

## V.

At noon I look
like what the world calls a woman.

I wander from the sky
on to roads warm with day,
see my arms brown with it.

By day I meet a creature
patient as the morning, and as kind,
with sun-sky eyes,
a gentle mouth.

I fall.

We wander graveyards, seashores,
talk of kings and cormorants,
hold each other's hands.

I tell my sun-bright creature
that in the dark, I glow.
I shine.

*But you are not in the dark,* observes my creature.

I speak of the beauty of the stars,
of my longing to wander always near them,
of how, though I am not a star,
I gleam like them
in the dark.

---

*You do not gleam with me*, says my creature.

I do. I do.
But you eclipse me.
You are so bright —
and you live within the day —
and you know nothing of the dark —
if I stay with you,
encircle you,
if I stay fallen in this place with you,
I will never be seen in the dark again,
never shine with stars again. *Just a phase,*
as if the moon did not have more than a face,
as if to orbit is to stand still —
*you're fixed now*
and
*you faked it*
and
*your light was our reflection.*

My creature's hands encircle my face,
shade it from the sun,
coax a shining from it:

*I am not afraid of the dark.*

## VI.

I used to think I was a star.

I used to think
*I am only visible at night.*

But, strange to find —
there are times in-between,
lights by which I can be seen.
I learn new words to tell my hours:
*dusk* and *dawn* and *twi* and *gloam*,
wander through them holding hands,
burning to be known.

Jeannelle Ferreira

## Ardat-Lilî

She wove the woman through the wych-elm;
She kissed the grand duchesses' cooling mouths.
And it was (she says) a century for children,
stacked and red-cheeked,
waiting for her, dressed for winter in a scattering of loam.

She lost her appetite for them.
Now, in your bed, she eats apples,
smearing honey. Between her breasts, (for irony) a ruby
trembles, as if she breathed. The year
turns at sunset, her knee
a sharp hook at your thigh, her fingers
chasing the scrape of her pointed teeth.

Inanna was easy (left her weeping);
modern girls, a brush of your hand
through lightning. She says it and smiles
at the hand-of-Miriam shielding your throat.
(her hands were sand-creased, her hair starless black.)
*That's pretty,* she tells you
and bends, in the dark of the bedroom, down to drink.

## Encantada

I slide from the muddy waters,
long nosed, pink skinned, rolling
into arms and legs, shaking on
uneven ground. The leaves
fall hard around me. I hush
your strangled cries with
fish, sweet fish, so free of salt,
the gifts of mud and water,
and rinse you in the sullen rains.
Use me, oh use me, sweet my child,
to sing your skin and swelling belly,
to shadow secrets filthier than mud,
to tell them you are sick of dreams
of muddied water and river waves,
to blame me for this coming child.
And do not tell them, sweet my child,
how you know, oh how you know,
you do not, cannot, bear my child.
You know: you suckled at my breasts
before I slid back beneath the heavy river
to bury your secrets deep in river mud.

*Lisa M. Bradley*

### we come together we fall apart

I. Abe

Three sisters, then.
It was easier that way.
You wouldn't think
so many mouths
could hold one secret.
But it was a big secret
and deadly.
Six sets of lips and teeth
barely kept the thrashing thing in check.
And what our mouths couldn't hold
we gripped tight in nails and fists.

We were a young man
let loose in the world
'cause Daddy wrapped his hands
'round Mama's neck
one last time
made fists we couldn't scrape away
so she closed her eyes
in red-rimmed relief
never woke again.
We ran, but for years
we dreamed we were still there
lip split and nails bloody
cowering in the corner of forever.

We would've been better
released into the wild
than that mining town.
But it was as far as our legs could run

—we only had two back then.
No wolves in woods or nightmare
were half so ravenous as
the miners' wives. They coal-eyed
our smooth skin, our clean and nimble fingers.
They stroked our back unbent
chewed our kisses
licked us hard and soft again.
They swallowed our seed like
sweet stinging whiskey
hotter than their husbands' ash.

Honest work was no use.
What fences could be mended
what wells dug
when those women uncurled
the hammer from our fist,
the shovel from our palm?
But they kept us clean and fed.
We would've kept their secrets forever
—no soot on the sheets—
had it not been for our own.

Remember: so big and wild and deadly
and still so new.
It needed to be held
between teeth; it needed
to be pinned to the ground
its ruff clenched in a master's grip...
kind of like we wanted *him*
to take us:
That man in the bar

—

with the cards in his hands
all hearts and spades
and the whiskey-shine in his eyes
his pick-axe jammed into our chest
cracking our ribs apart
to finger at our heart.


II. Marguerite

Three brothers, then.
At least
that's what they said.
And who would've doubted them
as alike as they were?
Like chokecherries boiled thrice
the red dye growing fainter every time.

We didn't align by age.
Adelita was in trouble
and she needed an older man
unhindered by whispers
to save her name.
Not to mention
even then, belly rounding
she wouldn't wed a man
who wouldn't bed her hard and regular.
So she took Abe
and I, the eldest
married the next, Micah.
Camille, our little sister
sang a song of gathering

before her vows with Connor
to bind us.

I never had children
but no matter
I'd always had my hands full
with Adelita
and now I had her babe.
(How the happy couple slept,
I'll never know;
many a night I trekked
the path between our houses
unable to ignore
poor Dolly's wailing
a minute more.)

And if Micah never quite looked at me
as Abe did Adelita
well, our farm had six new hands
eager for honest work, even
Micah's, despite his smooth, soft skin
his clean and nimble fingers.
And I had my pride:
Micah's back unbent
his neck supple as whiskey?
They were safe from whip and noose
because he married me
Saint Marguerite.

III. Micah

We still remember that man at the bar.
He knew how to hold a pick-axe
but he was the mine owner's son
so he never had need.
Those canny hands of his
cupped his cards, all spades and hearts
caressed the air and we watched
till the back of our neck burned
for his phantom yoke
our lap warmed for his leash.
He laughed
and the whiskey-loosed bitterness
tugged through our pants, made us
thicker and hotter than the gropings
of any greedy miner's wife.

A bar girl saved us
when words turned rough
when threats unraveled the thickness
overtaking the card table.
The other players tried to club us
and the owner's son, for we were
of a kind: eye to eye, hand to hand
axe to aching heart.
Shielded by his daddy's money
he dodged sledgehammer fists
and insinuation, did nothing
but fold his hand and tilt his chair
to watch the girl pull us upstairs
for our "appointment."

But once we reached her bedroom,
she shoved us at the window.
"Get gone if you love life,"
she said, "and don't come back.
No miner's son wants to see
his eyes in you
and no mine owner's son
will cry if you die
making rope-ripe eyes at him."

So again we ran as far as our legs
could carry us
—just two legs back then—
and we risked wolves and winter's wind
to sleep in the woods.
But rest outran our double-soul
and our darkness bulged with nightmares
long as the leash we trailed
and certain as a noose.


IV. Adelita

Some might've mistaken Micah
for the handsome one.
Marguerite sure did.
Never did a woman take such pride
in matters she had so little to do with.
The way she coddled my daughter
—forever carried her between our houses
though the men paved the path
door to door; before,

———
34

because Dolly's shoes would get muddy;
then, because she might slip on the stones.

Just so, she preened over Micah.
His supple neck
lighter lined than Abe's
his unbent back…
I caught Micah washing at the creek
more than once
watched the sun set fire to the water
coursing down his corded flesh
and it made me want
and wet down there
but his eyes, paler than Abe's
— like watered-down whiskey —
never reflected my flare, and I knew
he was not a man the whole way through.

Different women may be needing
different things.
By then I knew men do.
For someone like Saint Marguerite
I thought,
a fine view and a perfect kiss
might suffice, but the way she fussed
over his hands so smooth
his fingers clean and nimble…

My hands were always stained.
Marguerite's were thick as a man's
from shearing, knitting, and numbers
and Camille's danced like shape notes

ever braiding and unbraiding
her hair as she sang the flock
to pasture and back
but I was a mistress of color.
I seduced sepia from white birch
and scarlet from chokecherries.
I wooed cerulean from woad
and peridot from pigweed.

I wore my work like gloves
yet my gloved hands never failed
to work a man's magic.
Quite the contrary —
by constantly shedding colored disguise
my hands became quite sly.
One night I worked Abe thrice
and his wits came unwoven
his secrets unraveled
and he told me the truth.


*Abe's Interlude*

After several hours' crunching
our bed of cones and needles
we roped our shoes around our neck
and trekked into the river.
We slogged against its sawtooth current
embraced the numbness
spreading up our legs
—still only two then—
since it silenced our doubled soul

and staved off the weariness
that would not relent to sleep.

Only when the sun rose
did we see we were going east
and though that twist of river
angled upward, why, a lightness
lifted our shoulders!
It cracked open our chest
split our cloven soul.
And so strong was the sensation
of rising, of some weight shearing off
that we looked behind us
to see what we might've lost.

There was Micah,
as if our reflection had been
bullied back by the current.
But splashing, this shape fought
to keep pace with us.
We turned and struggled on
relieved to be divested of that one
who had yearned for the mine owner's son
(and others too, if truth be told).

He called to us to wait
but we crashed against the current
fists clenched, bare feet plunging
through the surface
into the second, sharper river
the colder one, deeper
that lurks within.

Another tap of the pick-axe
and a second weight slid free,
even as we, four-legged now
dredged up a third river.

We turned to see, not just Micah
and the soft silt we'd churned
into a current, but Connor too
(or three), lighter yet.
And who knows how many more
of us we might've jogged loose
had not that sight, as of
a fogged mirror cracked
shocked me so I spilled onto the verge
and Micah caught up with me
and Connor with him with me
and there we were, all three?
Six legs all'a sudden
but still not enough
to outrun our secret.


V. Connor

We never suspected three souls
hidden within our chest
but it seemed for the best
when we met the three sisters
with their limping-along sheep farm.
For we'd found no escape
from one another
— the pain of further separation

like a pick-axe to the skull—
and there was no re-fusing
—running west, with the currents,
always failed. So, much as Abe
wished to ditch Micah
and both of them estrange from me
we were three in one
one in three.

Camille was old enough to marry
but young enough to pale
at Abe and Adelita's passionate displays
naïve enough she didn't see
Micah and Marguerite's propriety
was its own display
akin to the way we played
house: our kisses little more
than bumped noses
our hands clasped rather than
our bodies, our baby
Adelita's.

I liked the sheep, who hovered
over the timothy grass like one
many-eyed, many-legged beast
attuned to the wind and Camille's songs.
Their ears flicked like shape notes
on a rustled page.
And I liked Camille, who corralled
the creatures with one song
set them free with another
who somehow harmonized

with herself, a choir of one.

Before we came, Camille pastured the sheep
with only her song, but after
she let me bring a shotgun
to warn off wandering dogs
the occasional coyote.
We'd saddle up a sheep for Dolly
another with our wrapped lunch
and set out for clover.
We'd return with the sun
chasing our long shadows to the door
and Camille's long braids
slapping her sturdy back.

When Micah went to town
to sell Adelita's bouquets of yarn
and Marguerite's knitting
we rode along, Camille and Dolly
jostling in the wagon.
While Micah attended to business
then vanished on "personal" errands
we lavished licorice and ribbon candy
on Dolly. We held her up to admire
the tinplate circus in the general store windows
held dresses up against
her wriggly body.

If Camille noticed
my headache-triggered temper
or Micah's mysterious new ease
on our journey home

she said nothing.
She sang though
the same harmony she used to weave
stray sheep into the flock
as she braided Dolly's
floss-fine hair.
More than once I wondered
if my relief truly came from reuniting
with Abe — who never smiled to see us —
or from Camille's gentle chorus
weaving our straggly family
together again.

One night before bed
Camille unwound her braids
by lamplight
and brushed her hair so long
it was like the locks had never
been separated, nor twisted
into trios. I worried what she was thinking
what weighty edict might lie
rope-ripe on her tongue
but then the sheep startled
and bleated and butted up against
the walls of their barn
till the wood creaked mutiny.

I rushed outside with shotgun
and Camille followed with lamp and song.
Micah and Marguerite soon joined us
Dolly in Micah's arms, and a rifle
in Marguerite's

and then Abe and Adelita
one gun and two blankets between them.
We lit more lamps and searched out
the threat, the sheep still thrashing
in their haven, but saw no sign
of bobcat or coyote, dog, fox or man.

While Camille soothed the flock
with arias of sleep and peace
we edged into the horizon
imagining wolves and notching guns
to tense shoulders. But nothing slunk
through the tall timothy grass or lurked
in tree-clumped shadows. The cicadas
and chorus frogs went silent
at nothing but our stomping feet.

We returned and Adelita grabbed Abe
with hands dyed whiskey-brown
from brewing goldenrod, and whipped him
down the path to their house
to finish their lusty fumbling.
Micah escorted wife and child indoors
but Camille lingered in the barn
still chanting at the nervous sheep.

I crept up and stroked the curtain
of hair from her face, asked her
to come inside. She turned into
my touch and asked
Was she a good wife?

## VI. Camille

I'd long loved Connor.
First, for the kindness in his eyes
though they were strange
like un-aged whiskey, clear and bright.
Then, for the mercy he showed me
making no demands of a girl
not ready for the marriage bed.
For the lightness of his touch
with Dolly and all small creatures.
For the sweet, simple rest he took
in my arms, in my song
on wagon rides home.

I never understood his brothers' scorn
their jokes about his faded hair
his white lightning eyes
his wrinkleless neck and slight form
especially since his everything
differed in degree not form
from their own. Yet perhaps
his gentle humor wore them down
or my song worked its spell.
For finally
they stopped ribbing, stopped snubbing
and one day Dolly and I
back from gathering goldenrod
found the three brothers struggling
to free a fat ewe from the slats
of a paddock
and all three were covered in mud

and laughing so hard, their guts ached
longer than the bruises
from her cloven kicks.

Only, even as Micah and Abe
accepted Connor
my sister Adelita turned against him.
To my shame, I first suspected
that she, in a moment hotblooded
had gotten too close
perhaps touched him as she did Abe
or looked at him the way
she did Micah, early on.
I could imagine it; it pecked at my heart
even though I knew
honorable Connor would guard
her pride and mine.

Not till the night of the sheep's panic
did I understand. The stink of fear
twined in my hair that moments before
I'd brushed so long it shone, while
Connor explained that though he loved me
he could not love me
as Abe did Adelita.
His eyes welled
more water than whiskey
by my trembling lamplight
and his pale mouth tightened
unwilling to let loose
some feral, fanged secret.

With cheeks ripe as chokecherries
I wondered at myself:
How could I hope to evoke
the passion Adelita brewed,
I with my childish braids
and skittish heart?
So I conjured from the dark
a shadow of a smile
and I tucked myself beneath
Connor's gentle white arm.
I let him lead me
home.

But seeing our bed with the woad-
embroidered sheets, my heart split open
and I could not bear to lie
beside a brother rather than a lover.
So I twined my fingers in his and said
"I know I've clung to youth too long
and it's no wonder you think me
more little sister than wife
but can we try? Maybe you can love me
at least a little bit?
Like Micah and Marguerite?"

His fingers fisted around mine
and I thought his supple neck
had tensed with fury.
But before my shock slid to panic
he shook his head and said
"Micah does not love Marguerite
not as a husband does a wife.

He hides behind her skirts
and grateful, performs as best he can.
But her apron strings are still a noose
for one who loves other men."

As if reading shape notes
I grasped his sense
before I understood his words
and I trembled, anticipating
the next verse, but Connor struck
a chord I couldn't foresee
explained my husband
— in name though not in deed —
desired neither man
nor woman
felt no burning of that kind.
He only wished I'd be his single friend
the way he begged to be mine.

I couldn't speak, no more than
I could pull out the phantom needle
piercing my heart
or maybe it was a pick-axe
the way the pain
cracked open my chest.
All I could do was scrape
his hand from mine
and run.

I crashed into the woods like a blind beast
snapping twigs loud as a herd of
clumsy cloven feet and startling

the choral frogs into silence.
Wild sobs unwound from
my mouth, endless as the lies
woven to trap me in this life.

My sisters must've known
how Connor differed
yet still they let me cleave to him
thinking only how neatly
this knotted all their loose ends:
Abe to absolve Adelita's sins
Marguerite to harbor Micah
Connor, my consolation,
and three new backs, strong and unbent
to prop our struggling farm.
Did they never think I'd want
what they had?
They'd been as careless of me
as with Dolly.

Part of me slept there in the pines
and part of me raved through the night and dawn
and yet another part
grew hungrier in my belly than
between my legs, but I refused to rise
from the marsh of my tears.
Connor didn't come for me.
Abe did, a smile on his lips
chiseled from stronger stuff.
And true, after years of Adelita
he was wiser in the ways
of luring wild-eyed women

from the ledge of ultimatum.

He knelt beside me, stroked my hair
his words timed to the soothing
passes of his smooth hands
two shades darker than Connor's
two wishes warmer…
"There, there, girl.
Don't cry no more.
Here's the morning and ain't nothing
we can't mend by its sweet light."
I twisted away and sobbed.
"Don't speak to me as if I'm Dolly
with a skinned knee. I'm married
to a man who can't love me
who can't bear to touch me
and you knew it, all of you."

Which was when Abe bent
and whispered near my ear
about knowing need
and what, if daring, we could do.


*Micah's Interlude*

Headache subsiding,
I sagged with relief
unseeing but knowing
Abe had returned, finally forfeiting
his wild-girl chase.
Camille had trudged home

near an hour before
and though she glared Connor into exile
—he slunk next door—
now she sucked honey and cornbread
from her fingers, while Marguerite
carded pine needles from her hair
and Dolly watched Adelita brew
walnut hulls for coal-black dye.

Abe opened the door and smote
one headache, only to ignite another.
I saw the sickened rage flare
from Camille's still-red eyes
and disgust pinched my lips,
mimicked Abe's mouth pursed
in silent threat.
I felt a fist in my throat, a stopper
of frustration fit to match
my clenched hands.
Abe's impulses: so pure and
sanctioned
and always pitching us
into thickets.

Saint Marguerite
by now well versed
as Dolly in let's pretend
was too engrossed in her carding work
to notice the storm surge
but Adelita…
her hands, drenched black
stopped stirring and she glanced

from Abe to Camille
and she understood his betrayal at once
verdict heavy
as a sledgehammer.

Camille fled
to the comfort of her sheep
or perhaps to comfort her sheep
for again they bleated and beat
their heads against the paddock
in unison: their wont whenever
unease ruffled Camille's spirit.
Abe and Adelita argued
with mouths more teeth than lips
and fewer words than kicks and fists.
Marguerite escaped under guise
of shielding Dolly from her parents' fury
but I, though not so fair as Connor
had fallen out of Adelita's sight
as well as favor
and Abe considered me
less than piss or shadow
so, ignored, I stayed and sipped
my coffee, let their repetition
drift me back
to old regrets.

The mine owner's son…
did his daddy's money still pull
the punches of suspicious drunks?
Or had his whiskey-bright eyes
gone dull as the dust on a hanged man's

---

shoes? Had he found saint's rest
like me? Had he nothing left to lose?


## VII. The Flock

The one called Adelita, she had black hands and a black web over
her heart that We have learned is called *hate* and is knit from bright
barbed wire (*vanity*) and begging, bloody wool (*hurt*). The Adelita
threatened to **leave** us and the songs We sang in the backs of our
brains stopped, as still as the chorus frogs when they sense the
shadows with teeth and claws. For long ago We were *separate:* some
had arms and legs and eyes they called their own and they
wandered from the flock and were lost, only they called it *freedom*
and thought it sweet. But the Adelita was already lost, had
forgotten the binding song, and her threat was thunder drowning
the notes that shaped our flock.

In the Adelita's arms fought the small one, much loved by all, she
who rode with us and smelled of sticky ribbons and climbed the
separate arms and legs, and she was called Dolly for her smallness
and how she was passed around. The one called saint and
Marguerite wept, which is like rain but bitter, and the one called
Micah reached for the Dolly, who reached back. But the Adelita
kept the Dolly trapped in arms like paddock locks and howled what
is Truth: that even longer ago, the many were one. Only her hate-
laced heart spoke to hurt not heal us, and this made the one called
Abe roar and run at the Adelita with hands clenched into fists,
which is a way of turning many into one also, but still to hurt not to
heal.

Yes, it is awful all the things We did when We were not We but Them.

The one called Camille ran from the paddock and We followed her, for even then We sensed her sameness and would be where she was. We saw the Abe squeeze his fists around the Adelita's throat to stop the words from coming out — words are broken bits of song that sink and fall and sometimes pull the world down with them — and there was much screaming — which is words pushed past song and shattered. The Dolly, still in arms, she was not screaming but singing a song of gathering — she had learned the harmonies from the Camille — only her voice was small and the tune lonely and the separate ears would not hear.

Finally the one called Connor, beloved of Camille, he made a thicket of himself and pushed between the Adelita and the Abe. He fought to scrape fists from throat. But then the Dolly fell and there was a shattering inside her. The one called Camille shared the shattering and we ran to catch her on our huddled backs. But she did not fall, though her song fell silent under ache.

Our many hearts beat many notes. We were afraid.

Unknowing, the others rushed to lift the small one, while the Camille thought scarlet thoughts of things we did not understand, like *pick-axes* and *knitting needles*, *sledgehammers* and *shotguns*, until her ache gave way to screams. But, like ours, the Camille's throat was not formed for screams, and with our muzzles nudging, she quick pushed past the shattering inside her to sing a new song, a song of healing. Like the whispering of wind over clover, it had no words, only verses. But the song was round — *never leaving, never letting go* — and the chorus was *Forever*.

52

*Connor's Epilogue*

We are here. We are a part, apart. We remember no names but *Camille*. We have long loved Camille.

We will not say "in our own way." Love *is* the way.

We are some of us restless. Even now, we remember other bodies and make skirmishes in our self. But We are strong enough to break the bonds of wood and wire, broad enough to raze the meadows. Together, We are free.

There are other flocks who roam the valleys, and they look like us but they bolt from us for they are not like us. We carry a strange bouquet. We reek of coal and whiskey, licorice and lust, chokecherries and woad, wolf and rope and rust.

We age and die. We bear and grow. But our number is no matter. There is no *I* or *him*, *her* or *them*, *me* or *you* to know.

Sometimes the wind carries our song. We feel it on our muzzles and in our blood, looped through our wool, like a leash we've come to love. We can no longer sing, lyrics useless to our tongues, but we have no need: We *are* the song.

## The Gabriel Hound

On the first night the Moongirl comes to Kir as she and the hound slip over and under the invisible trails between root and ground. Breathless and rounding an oak gnarled with years and smoke-dark under shade and moonlight, dog and girl run together. *She* is there, small and lithe, a supple twist of moonbeam and muscled like the dog, a feral thing like a scrap of white porcelain.

"Come," she calls, lifting a leper-pale hand to the hound, who bares her teeth and backs her haunches against girlflesh. Kir puts chapped fingers against dogflesh and sings beneath her breath:

> Little dog, little dog
> brindle and white,
> the storm's in the cellar
> moon taking flight.
> Stay with me always,
> be never away,
> guard me at midnight,
> I'll keep watch by day.

> (when the storm broke and Kir and her father walked the borders and the outbuildings, checking the weave of rowan through the latches, the goats were whole and the cattle were unbled, but a whisper of a white pup sat before the barn doors)

On the second night the Whip comes to Kir as she and the hound slip over and under the invisible trails between root and ground. Breathless and rounding an oak gnarled with years and smoke-dark under shade and moonlight, dog and girl run together. *He* is there, lean and cruel and clever, clad in thin ropes that wind his limbs and pinch his flesh into peak and valleys.

"Come," he commands, his voice a crack of leather, and the hound quivers and lays her trembling chin on the girl's knee. Kir gasps and lifts the dog's ear:

> Little dog, hunter's hound
> hound of my heart,
> stay close beside me
> and never we'll part.
> Shape of a woman
> please you to take,
> I'll tread lonesome byways,
> For my true love's sake.

> > (Kir's father loved the beast not, but fed it its fill, for he knew the hunt would return expecting its hound well-grown and ready for the chase)

On the third night the Lady of Shadows comes to Kir as she and the hound slip over and under the invisible trails between root and ground. Breathless and rounding an oak gnarled with years and smoke-dark under shade and moonlight, dog and girl run together. *She* is there, tall and dark as the heart of smoke, like an armful of sky torn from the night and made into the shape of a woman. In the soft folds of her gown jewels spangle like stars.

"Come," she whispers, and this is the worst, for her voice is woodsmoke and fernseed, and the hound whimpers and thrusts her nose beneath the girl's arm. Kir chokes on salt and stutters:

> Little dog, lover dog,
> made for the chase,

made for the quarry
and Oberon's race.
You will be master, and
I will be least.
If you can't be human,
I shall be beast.

> (she let the little dog into her bed one night, for it
> cried beside the fire, and in the morning it took
> meat from her hand and her father knew, and
> her sister wept)

The Moongirl bays and the Whip welts blood from Kir's hide and
the Lady smiles, in pity if the Hunt could feel pity, and Kir runs
with the storm and flinches at rowan and sleeps tangled with the
pack. She knows she is ill made for the life; she doesn't care. She
will not last the year. Her father and sister have buried her old
straw doll in lieu of her; they know she won't return. Should
another pup appear her father will kill it, come what may. He will
not lose another daughter.

*Alexandra Seidel*

## A Masquerade in Four Voices

Come, Mother, braid my hair. My dress hangs ready on its frame, emeralds entwined in silk, turquoise sea wrangled free from merfolk's grasp and purples rich as plums. I have waited for this dress long, oh so long and my hair has grown for it, is ready to be woven like sheep wool on a loom, is ready to become a tower under your hands, is willing to shine. Darken my eyes with kohl at last and drain into my lips the richness of apricots. Kiss me one last time, Mother, and mold the mask to my skin; I am ready now to go to the

Balls are made halfway at least in dreams. This, my child, is one of their many secrets. Also, beneath the silk and brocade and the shimmering masks, these are really just humans, mostly anyways. I have worn the mask of jokers in many a dream, but I should think that the King of Time is a first for you, is it not? Scarlet suits you, after all, you look quite the gentleman prize. Let nobody ever tell you that you do not

Belong to this feast, this festivity, this magic, for just one night! Who with the breath still in their lungs could not want this? The young ones are so eager, the veterans distinguished and those who only visit for the night, well, they are quite

Choosing one of them to dance with you, to hold them close and let their lace lick my footsteps' echo on the dance floor, there is nothing quite as sweet as this. Of course the lace and silk are only half the price paid for dancing here, the shoes of silver glass only part of the subtlety required. Whatever happens while the moon is in the sky, nobody ever parts with their

Masks everywhere, like echoes of rain in the mountains. Mother, if only you could see this! I have left home, but feel like I am home

57

again among the candlelight and the frankincense in the air, among the masks of eagles and of sorcerers, unicorns and lions, birds with plumage red as

Blood is so sought after. You must understand this. It is a ball, a masquerade after all, and thus as much a hunt as all of these things put together. All of them want to draw first blood, thinking that it will make them brave and exulted, but they fail to realize that this first bead of ruby may be their own. So, you see, while scarlet suits you, it also condemns you, King of Time, to the longing in their

Eyes are ever on you here. They must be, or else this would not be a ball that could hold those of my standing amongst the heavens, not even for the space of a cup of wine. Mine is the mask of the Hunter, my bow already in my hand. Once I have set my eyes on you it really is just a matter of

Time is my kingdom, just for this night; if I could though, I would stretch it out like soft dough under my fingers, grind your smile into every little grain my hourglasses hold. My Lotus Queen, will you give me this

Dance, dance, this will be like a hunt through the woods, a fugue in the darkness! My fingers feel your heartbeat under them quickening already, my bow string tightens. I release my arrow straight into your heart like a gift, see it hit the center with a vibrato of

Violins were ringing in my ears then, oh Mother! His hand hot against mine one moment then softly pried away by the stranger in the mask of green and crimson. Everybody turned and stared, the dance stopped for just the fraction of a note; people bowed to the crimson masked stranger, cradling my Time King to his chest. But it is just like this for those who dance this ball, the dancers

Change never, my sweet boy. The others, look at them! dance this roundelay for years, from the day their feet can hold the shoes to the day their bones will no longer sing with the melody, hoping all the time to find themselves as lucky as I have made you. You are mine now, and I yours, after a fashion. Come, my sweet boy, let your scarlet silk trickle along my hands like a tongue wet with hunger. Follow me, you will be the King of Time forevermore. Never let anybody tell you that you were not ready to pay the

Price.

Sonya Taaffe

# Persephone in Hel

Half her face is rotted grain.
Through dry wheat withies,
the daub and grate of her ribs,
the pomegranate smolders,
a red sun at the rim of a winter field.
To kiss her is the spade's slice
into grave-goods, the late earth scattering
sockets, teeth, fibula pins.
To slip into her is digging for poppies.
She reaches in me for famine and the knife.
We fall on the threshold
in dying flowers and frozen dew,
our faces laid together a single facade.
You look at us and see two deaths entangled,
but between us there is always room for you.

*Sergio Ortiz*

## Rain and Sound

*Listen to me as one listens to the rain:*
we are distracted once again.  Night
approaches with its dense cloak of fear,
an assault for which there is no cure.
It is never winter here,
yet the hibiscus have been censored
like men trying to show their affection
for each other.  Air, water, and flower —
there is no weight in these words.
Night has the figurations of mist.
*Listen to me as one listens to the rain:*
(Censor my desire for writing you poems.)
Not attentive, not distracted, only as if
I were the rain.  Hear me out until
the asphalt is wet.  You are you
in night steam.  You enter my eyes
as your steam crosses the street.
We are both steam.  Steam of another
censored flower.

*Sonya Taaffe*

# The Clock House

"Be kind, resourceful, beautiful, friendly, have initiative, have a
sense of humour, tell right from wrong, make mistakes, fall in love,
enjoy strawberries and cream … do something really new."
 — Alan Turing, "Computing Machinery and Intelligence" (1950)


Come ghost out of the machine, Christopher,
the clouds are gathering in Cheshire and Aquila
and beyond the darkening lens
the last of the boy-martyrs are being put to bed
with a glass of milk and an apple,
immaculate faces sweetly sleeping out
wars, plagues, apologies.
Here is Prospero of the decision problem
who drowned his books in cyanide
and his wanly smiling Ariel,
long freed from the equivocations of flesh,
the absent-minded atheist and his good angel
haloed with the sun in hindsight
over Canal Street and a saint's blue shoulder —
Christopher, as if you never fought
or fucked in Alan's muddled, book-racked room
between the bicycle clips and the chess notations,
Ravel's concerto crackling on the 78
that late, wet spring of '32.
You took Wittgenstein's classes and a double First
and wrote of numbers as real as identities,
irrational, integral and complex,
a light-lashed theorist with a dark, diffident glance,
not talking of night gasps or sunlit, starch-white beds.
He was your runner, bearing back like laurels
the hot smudge of lakeland heather

---

or the breakneck shiver of Sark's summer waves,
your pillow book of the night-lit ward,
reading his dark hair with sweating fingers
until your fever broke and no one's heart with it.
He sent punch-cards for postcards,
his war work as vague
as yours was a simple arithmetic
of empty seats and chalk-cold afternoons,
the endless subtracting of Cambridge,
stained glass, coal, and undergraduates.
You thieved his tea-mug
off its chain each time, a pair of profs
to choose between — the thin twist of wrists
like piano wire, a static crackle of a laugh —
unbreakable cipher and key of Dilly's Grecian eye.
Your parents met him at the graveside,
hatless and mannerless, an old page of fixed stars
fisted in his pocket like a ring.
Your daughters met him on Market Street,
their shabby, alchemical half-uncle
who bought them ice-creams
and told them the story of *Snow White*
and maybe still, long before you, died.
This is where you disappear, Christopher,
the vanishing point Alan ran to
as his program was pulled from its tapes.
What can I construe from a letter, a photograph?
The body is safe as glass houses,
the mind a black box.
I can smash these screens, but I cannot know you
any more than a message from the unseen world —
the dead who are noise and incalculable

and memory the most passing machine of all,
Christopher, unless you come to tell me
of a slow twilight on the Cam, of two voices talking drowsily
of Delphinus and von Neumann, central limits, cinema,
saying *no, but look here,* meaning love.

*Peter Milne Greiner*

## The Earth Has Rings

Hey his mouth does stutter afieldly

passable clearance when pulled on
like drawstrings   We nightly concoct

this patois from such scratch as limbs
provide; we umpire and replicate,
I pantomime his treesap pulse and wonder

so succinctly where talk hides at times
like this, when every second capsizes like

leaves before downpour and alphabets
thrive and die off between them, when
these routine ambuscades begin in the

diaphragm, end in accelerations, dishevel
further that sophisticated gibberish

we murmur like stamina into each other

*Adrienne J. Odasso*

## Parallax

Black hole at the heart
of Sagittarius: not fish
enough to be Capricorn,
not land-locked enough
to hunt. My paradox
is to be ever at the cusp,
never one / never other,
grasping threads of each.

You called me *boy*,
and I smiled to know
my chimerical self
was untouchable;

you called me *girl*,
and I marvelled at how
it is to move between
worlds, ever guessing

what you will say next.

*Tori Truslow*

# Terrunform

We came trained to turn the land on
to the sun's look, teach this world to be ours;
as others dress the hills — smart-lichen to blush
hot green across cold red — we drill the shining
soil, and slowly, in these thrice-stretched
summers, it Marsforms us.

See the forecasts we send back:
new curls of continent, the planet tempered
by our toil, just like home — but in these days we slough
off our soft flesh; I rebuild you, and you rebuild me
in these nights that unfix us, these skies
that rewire us, copper and light —

and remember what we said
young girls with red star-stoked eyes?
It wasn't new Earth we wanted, but to be
double-mooned, double-dreamed, multiformed in
mix-matched parts; to put our bodies on
each day, in shapes to fit our hearts

— and the red-gazy girls that
stand there still, and see this star
engreened, should know: how we twist
in the thinner grip of this gravity, how space
is the roar in our wires, and how I look past your
shoulder out to the black, and scratch a rocket into your back.

*Peer G. Dudda*

## Sister Dragons

Sister dragons, your beautiful wings!
They cringe, call your flesh scaly,
Ignorant of your graceful flight,
A dance spun full of truth.
My wings were chopped off,
An attempt to ground me under heel:
Keep me timid, keep me docile, full of fear, full of shame,
Taught me to cut myself every time growth buds appeared.

Sister dragons, never did it occur to me
That like you, I could put down the knife and rasp,
Put away the gauze and antiseptic,
Let the wings grow back,
Join you in flight,
Until now.

Watch these gracile wings grow.
One day they will spread, gossamer membranes ready
To push against air and fly home.

# About the Contributors

Mary Alexandra Agner writes of dead women, telescopes, and secrets in poetry, prose, and Ada. Her latest book is *The Scientific Method*. She has observed the universe her whole life and written about it. She can be found online at www.pantoum.org.

"Tertiary" is one of the most personal poems I've ever written, sprung entirely from my own wish to be rid of anatomy that has always made me the focus of unwanted attention and which I'm never going to use for its intended purpose. The word play and slangy diction employed in the poem are my attempt to keep the subject matter at bay.

Michele Bannister was born in the year of Halley's Comet, and retains an uncommon fondness for distant worlds both small and icy. She lives in Australia, where she is working towards her doctorate in astronomy. Her poetry has also appeared in *Strange Horizons* and *Cascadia Subduction Zone*, and is forthcoming in *Jabberwocky*, *Ideomancer* and *inkscrawl*.

She was inspired to write "Seamstress" after reading of the women who created the individually fitted spacesuits of the Apollo program.

Lisa M. Bradley's poetry, ranging from haiku to epic, has appeared in numerous venues, including *Strange Horizons*, *Mothering*, *Weird Tales*, and *The Moment of Change* anthology.

"we come together we fall apart" arose from her interests in the multiplicity of self, sibling marriages (brothers from one family marrying sisters from another), art communes, and complex family structures. The poem was also heavily inspired by her newest love: gothic country music. Lisa blogs at cafenowhere.livejournal.com. You can also find her on Twitter and Tumblr, @cafenowhere.

Peer G. Dudda is a deaf queer immigrant who lives in suburban Minneapolis with a significant other and an overactive imagination. Tech support may pay the bills, but language feeds the soul, especially the lexical gaps found across the mind's landscape, which are really furrows in which to sow seeds of poetry. Peer's poetry appears in *Stone Telling* 1 and 7.

Amal El-Mohtar is an Ottawa-born Lebanese-Canadian, currently pursuing a PhD in the UK. She is a two-time winner of the Rhysling Award for Best Short Poem, and has been nominated for the Nebula award. She is the author of *The Honey Month*, a collection of poetry and prose written to the taste of twenty-eight different kinds of honey; her poems have also appeared in multiple venues online and in print, including *Stone Telling*, *Mythic Delirium*, and *Apex*. She also edits *Goblin Fruit*, an online quarterly dedicated to fantastical poetry. You can find her online at amalelmohtar.com.

Jeannelle Ferreira's recent work can be found in *Not One of Us* #47, *Steam-Powered II: More Lesbian Steampunk Stories* (Torquere Press), *The Moment of Change: Feminist Speculative Poetry* (Aqueduct Press) and *Stone Telling*. She realizes that Lilith is probably bored with the whole idea of human sexuality, but Lilith is proof that the Other has been with us from the beginning, and living as the Other, as a transgressive, queer, daring being – in the frum world or the secular – has its own particular delights.

Peter Milne Greiner is a poet and reviewer whose work also appears in *Fence*, *Diner Journal*, *FAQNP*, *eXiT sTraTa*, and *You're Beautiful, New York*. He is a co-creator of DrunknSailor, an ensemble reading series and maker of event-specific publications currently in residence at This Must Be The Place in Brooklyn. He is the author, with Anna Dunn, of the chapbook *Glyph Test Site*, a companion to the work of M. Mel Shimkovitz.

Hel Gurney grew up in rural Oxfordshire, studied in London, and is now in Brighton pursuing a postgraduate degree in gender-transgression and literature. Hel is fascinated by borders and binaries, memories and mythologies, and how they can be blurred and transcended. Appearing so far in *False Moustache* and *Stone Telling*, Hel's poetry roams across time, space, and genre. A committed activist, Hel also operates queer-feminist promotions label The Cutlery Drawer (thecutlerydrawer.org.uk). She is online at helgurney.wordpress.com

"Hair" is about rewriting the narratives that other people apply to my body. Does waist-length hair need to emblematise a sort of mythic femininity? Mine means other things to me, and cutting it won't make me more queer – just less myself.

Samantha Henderson's poetry has been published in *Strange Horizons*, *Goblin Fruit*, *Chizine*, and *Mythic Delirium*, and she is the co-winner of the 2010 Rhysling award for long poetry. Her first poetry collection, *The House of Forever*, will be released in 2012 from Raven Electrick Ink.

Shira Lipkin is a writer, activist, mother, and nexus. She has managed to convince *Electric Velocipede*, *Chizine*, *Interfictions 2*, *Mythic Delirium*, and other otherwise-sensible magazines and anthologies to publish her short fiction and poetry. She lives in Boston with her family and the requisite cats, fights crime with the Boston Area Rape Crisis Center, is taking suggestions for her burlesque name, does six impossible things before breakfast, and would like a nap now. You can track her movements at shiralipkin.com and shadesong.livejournal.com. Please do. She likes the company.

Alex Dally MacFarlane lives in London, where the foxes cross paths with her at night. Her work has appeared or is forthcoming in *Clarkesworld Magazine*, *Strange Horizons*, *Beneath Ceaseless Skies*, *The Mammoth Book of Steampunk*, *The Moment of Change* and *Stone Telling*. A handbound limited edition of her story "Two Coins" was published by Papaveria Press in 2010. She keeps a website at alexdallymacfarlane.com

"Sung Around Alsar-Scented Fires" is a song from the Tuvicen, one of many peoples who have settled another star system in the far-future. Alex is currently writing a novella about a young Tuvicen woman called Mar-teri.

Jack H. Marr is an English writer, craftsman and recovering lawyer living in Montreal, where he hopes to one day learn to understand Canadians better. As an immigrant, a witch, a fey bisexual, a disabled person, a fem man, a male who was assigned female at birth, he knows a bit about the queer skill of moving between worlds and living at intersections. He spends much of his time wrangling reptiles, caring for his loved ones, and skirmishing with bureaucracy. His writing has previously been published in *Gender and Transgender in Modern Paganism* and *Mytholog* magazine.

"Lunectomy" is his first poetry publication and arises out of his experience of transition-related surgery, gendered symbolism and (re)claiming his body and self.

Mari Ness has a fascination with water and creatures of the river and the sea. Her work has appeared in multiple publications, including *Clarkesworld Magazine*, *Apex Magazine*, *Strange Horizons*, and *Goblin Fruit*. For more links to her work, check out her webpage at marikness.wordpress.com, or follow her on Twitter @mari_ness.

Adrienne J. Odasso's poetry has appeared in a wide variety of strange and wonderful publications, including *Sybil's Garage*, *Mythic Delirium*, *Jabberwocky*, *Cabinet des Fées*, *Midnight Echo*, *Not One of Us*, *Dreams & Nightmares*, *Goblin Fruit*, *Strange Horizons*, *Stone Telling*, and *The Moment of Change* anthology. Her short fiction has also appeared both online and in print. Her two chapbooks, *Devil's Road Down* and *Wanderlust*, are available from Maverick Duck Press. Her first full collection, *Lost Books*, was released by Flipped Eye Publishing in April 2010.

"Parallax" is the first in a sequence of poems exploring the intersection of queer and intersex identities, as well as reflecting on having grown up without words (until relatively recently) for either one.

Sergio Ortiz is a retired educator, poet, painter, and photographer. Flutter Press released his chapbooks *At the Tail End of Dusk* and *Bedbugs in My Mattress*. Ronin Press released his third chapbook *topography of a desire* in May of 2010. Avantacular Press released his first photographic chapbook *The Sugarcane Harvest*. He is a three-time nominee for the Sundress *Best of the Net Anthology* and a Pushcart nominee.

Dominik Parisien lives in French, writes in English and dreams in a combination of the two. He is an intern for Cheeky Frawg Books and a former editorial assistant for *Weird Tales*. His poetry is forthcoming in *Star*Line* and has appeared in *inkscrawl* and *Stone Telling*.

"In His Eighty-Second Year" was his first published poem and emerged out of his experience working with the elderly.

Alexandra Seidel is a poet, writer, and editor who owns the mask of Joker. She has a powerful affection for the unreal and strange, the weird, the wicked, and naturally, the beautiful. Alexa loves speculative writing because that's where all these things come together with the power to create universes.

"A Masquerade in Four Voices" just came over her, fully formed and wanting to be written. It also appears in Alexa's first book, *All Our Dark Lovers*, to be released on Valentine's Day 2013 from Morrigan Books.

Nancy Sheng was born in northern China and raised in a ragtag fashion across Canada and the U.S. She is currently a graduate student in library sciences at the University of Toronto. On sunny days she likes to lounge in bed and take naps. Coincidentally this is also what she enjoys doing on wintry days. She is told her excessive fondness for being unconscious is a queer thing, but then again, so is she.

Sonya Taaffe's short stories and poems have appeared in such venues as *The Moment of Change: An Anthology of Feminist Speculative Poetry*, *People of the Book: A Decade of Jewish Science Fiction & Fantasy*, *Last Drink Bird Head*, *The Year's Best Fantasy and Horror*, *The Alchemy of Stars: Rhysling Award Winners Showcase*, *The Best of Not One of Us*, and *Trochu divné kusy 3*. Her work can be found in the collections *Postcards from the Province of Hyphens* and *Singing Innocence and Experience* (Prime Books) and *A Mayse-Bikhl* (Papaveria Press). She is currently on the editorial staff of *Strange Horizons*; she holds master's degrees in Classics from Brandeis and Yale and once named a Kuiper belt object.

"Persephone in Hel" was written for Lila Garrott-Wejksnora in December 2010.

"The Clock House" is for Christopher Morcom (July 13 1911 – February 13 1930) and Alan Turing (June 23 1912 – June 7 1954). The reasons are different, but they should both have had more life.

Bogi Takács is a confusingly gendered Hungarian Jewish woman. Her native language has no gendered personal pronouns and she wishes Spivak pronouns would see wider adoption in English. For the time being she has a hard enough time convincing people to spell her name with an acute accent. She mostly writes nonfiction for Hungarian magazines. (Topics frequently requested by editors: Nazis, occultism, and cute little animals.) Her English-language speculative poetry has been published in *Astropoetica* and is forthcoming in *Comets and Criminals*.

Tori Truslow was born in Hong Kong, grew up in Bangkok and now lives and writes in England, on a hill overlooking the place where the Thames meets the sea. Tori's poetry has appeared in *Goblin Fruit* and *Stone Telling*, is upcoming in *Penning Perfumes*, and has been performed at festivals and spoken word events across the UK.

"Terrunform" grew out of a desire to see more space narratives where gender isn't necessarily binary, and bodies don't have to define us. Visit toritruslow.com to find out more.

# About the Stone Bird Team

Rose Lemberg lived on the Ukrainian/Polish border, in subarctic Russia, and in Israel before moving to the US to become a graduate student at UC Berkeley. Some years later she defended her dissertation and moved to the Midwest, where she at last officially became an immigrant. She works as an assistant professor at a local university. Rose started writing in English in late 2007 and her stories and poetry have appeared in *Fantasy, Jabberwocky, Strange Horizons, Beneath Ceaseless Skies, Goblin Fruit, Apex* and other venues. In 2011 her queer epic poem "In the Third Cycle" won the Rannu competition.

She is the founder and co-editor (with Shweta Narayan) of *Stone Telling*, a magazine of boundary-crossing speculative poetry. Rose also edited *The Moment of Change*, the first-ever anthology of feminist speculative poetry, for Aqueduct Press (May 2012). Rose is currently hard at work on two novels and a chapbook about queer shapechangers. Find her online at roselemberg.net.

Jennifer Smith thinks having a bio is antithetical to hiding behind the perfect alias she was born to, but she does enjoy working behind the scenes to produce beautiful issues of *Stone Telling, inkscrawl,* and now this chapbook. She finds obsessing over margins, spelling and punctuation to be soothing, although she feels HTML is infinitely preferable to Word and may spring for a copy of InDesign soon.

Stone Bird Press is Rose's first foray into print publishing – and *Here, We Cross* is the first Stone Bird title. This press is something of an experiment; two titles are coming out in 2012, with both being collections of *Stone Telling* poetry. What kind of eggs will the stone bird lay in 2013? It is too early to tell. Visit us at stonebirdpress.com for updates and announcements.

20586493R00056

Printed in Poland
by Amazon Fulfillment
Poland Sp. z o.o., Wrocław